It's Not Catching

Burns & Blisters

Angela Royston

www.heinemann.co.uk/library
Visit our website to find out more information about **Heinemann Library** books.

To order:
☎ Phone 44 (0) 1865 888066
🖹 Send a fax to 44 (0) 1865 314091
💻 Visit the Heinemann Bookshop at www.heinemann.co.uk/library to browse our catalogue and order online.

First published in Great Britain by Heinemann Library, Halley Court, Jordan Hill, Oxford OX2 8EJ, part of Harcourt Education. Heinemann is a registered trademark of Harcourt Education Ltd.

Editorial: Sarah Eason and Kathy Peltan
Design: Dave Oakley, Arnos Design
Picture Research: Helen Reilly, Arnos Design
Artwork: Tower Designs UK Ltd
Production: Edward Moore

Originated by Dot Gradations Ltd
Printed and bound in Hong Kong and China by South China Printing Company

The paper used to print this book comes from sustainable sources.

ISBN 0 431 02148 1
08 07 06 05 04
10 9 8 7 6 5 4 3 2 1

British Library Cataloguing in Publication Data
Royston, Angela
Burns and blisters. – (It's not catching)
617.1'1

A full catalogue record for this book is available from the British Library.

Acknowledgements
The publishers would like to thank the following for permission to reproduce photographs: Alamy/Image Source p. **23**; Alamy/Image100 p. **12**; Comstock p. **8**; Getty Images p. **20**; Getty Images/Brian Stablyk p. **28**; Getty Images/Davies & Starr pp. **9**; Getty Images/Stephanie Rausser p. **25**; John Birdsall p. **27**; Last Resort Photo Library p. **26**; Mediscan p. **17**; Mica B Photography p. **10**; Phillip James Photography pp. **11, 22, 24, 29**; SPL/Chris Priest p. **6**; SPL/Dr P Marazzi pp. **5, 19**; SPL/Mark Clarke pp. **13, 14**; Trevor Clifford pp. **4, 7, 15**; Tudor Photography p. **21**.

Cover photograph reproduced with permission of Trevor Clifford.

The publishers would like to thank David Wright for his assistance in the preparation of this book.

Every effort has been made to contact copyright holders of any material reproduced in this book. Any omissions will be rectified in subsequent printings if notice is given to the publishers.

Contents

Words written in bold, **like this**, are explained
in the Glossary

What are burns and blisters?

A **burn** is what happens to your skin when it is damaged by something very hot. Hot objects, hot liquid, **steam** or strong sunshine can all burn your skin.

4

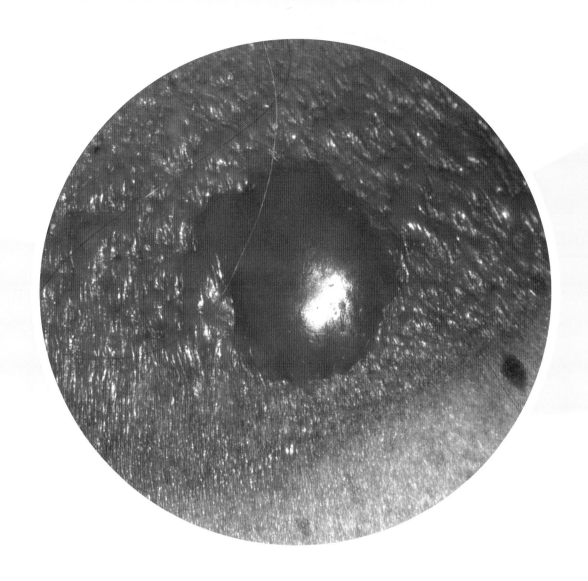

A **blister** is a bubble of liquid that forms at the surface of your skin when it has been burned. The blister protects the damaged skin below it.

Who gets burns and blisters?

You cannot catch a **burn** or **blister** from someone else. Most burns are caused by **accidents** that happen in the home or at work, especially when people are cooking.

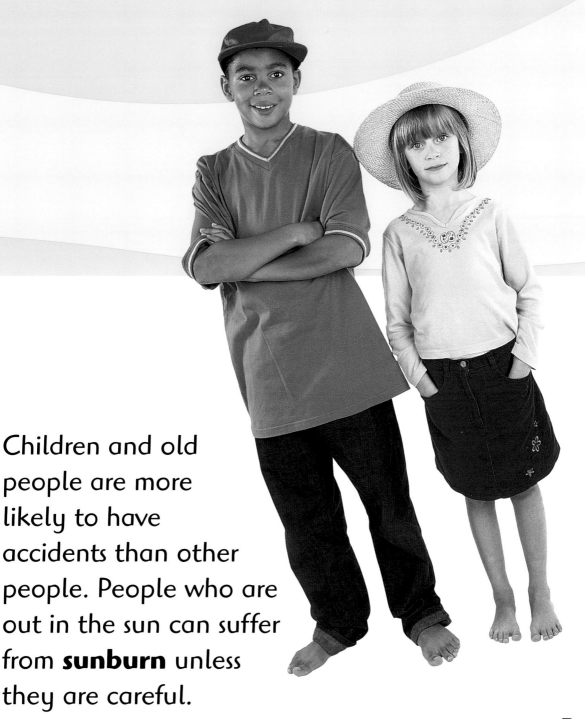

Children and old people are more likely to have accidents than other people. People who are out in the sun can suffer from **sunburn** unless they are careful.

Hot objects

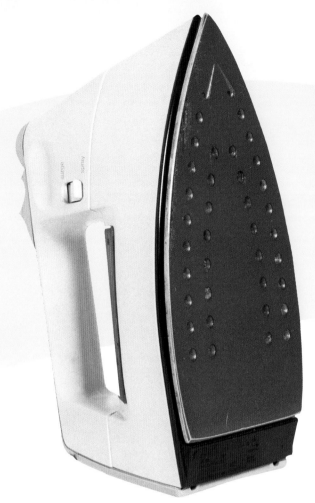

Many **electrical appliances** become **burning** hot when they are on. Irons, ovens and hobs become very hot. They stay hot for a while after they have been switched off.

Matches, candles, fires, barbecues and other things that are burning are very hot too. They are hot enough to burn wood and coal, so they are hot enough to burn skin!

Hot liquids and steam

Hot liquids and **steam scald** you. A scald is the same as a **burn**. A very hot bath or shower can scald you, and so can a hot drink.

A boiling hot drink scalds your tongue and the inside of your mouth. Boiling water makes steam, and steam is even hotter than boiling water!

Sunburn

The sun does not feel as hot as many other things, but it can **burn** your bare skin. When you are busy, you may not realize that the sun is burning you.

Sunburn may happen quite quickly or may take several hours. Sunburn makes your skin red. A few hours later, the burnt skin feels hot and sore.

What causes blisters?

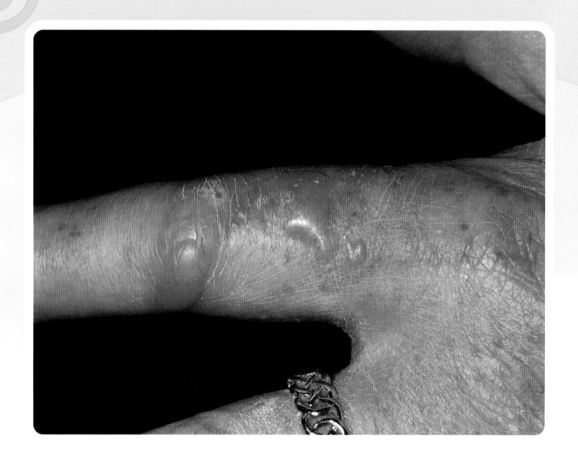

Some **blisters** are caused by **burns**. The blister helps to protect the skin while it **heals**. Other blisters are caused by something rubbing on a small patch of your skin.

New shoes are
stiff and may rub
your **heel** or another
part of your foot. If
your shoes are very worn,
they may rub your skin too.

Inside a blister

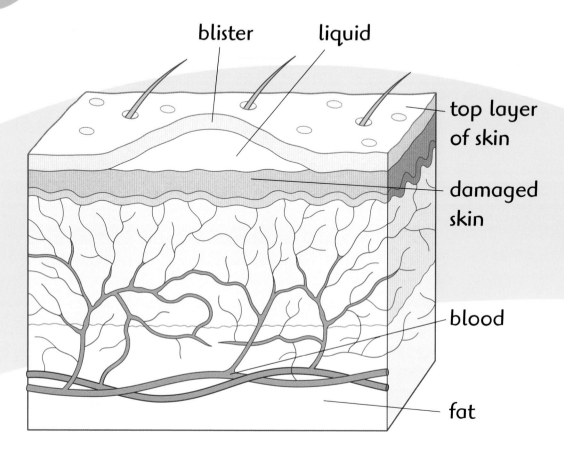

blister   liquid

top layer of skin

damaged skin

blood

fat

A **blister** is filled with liquid that is made by your body. The liquid forms a cushion between the top layer of skin and the delicate skin under it.

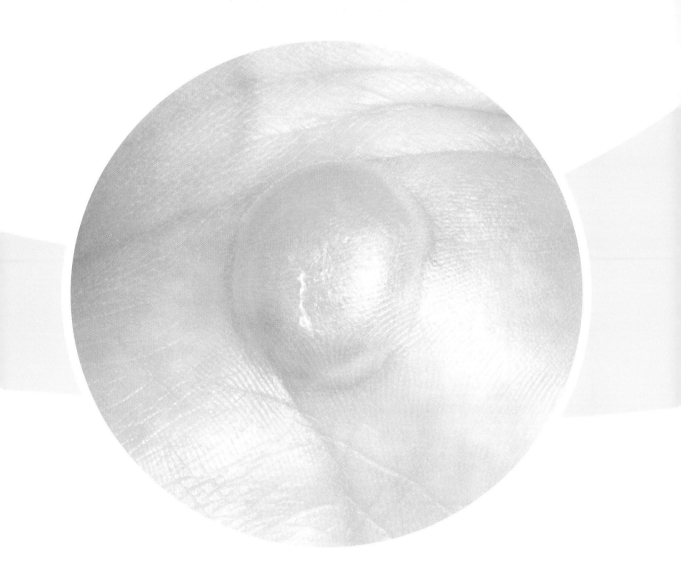

Do not prick a blister or try to burst it in other ways. As the blister **heals**, the liquid slowly drains away into your blood.

Damaged skin

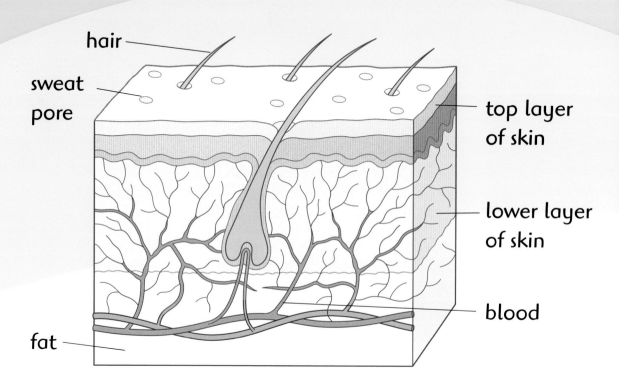

hair

sweat pore

top layer of skin

lower layer of skin

blood

fat

Burns are painful because they damage your skin. A deep burn that affects the lower layer of skin is more serious than one that affects just the top layer. This is what your skin looks like under the surface.

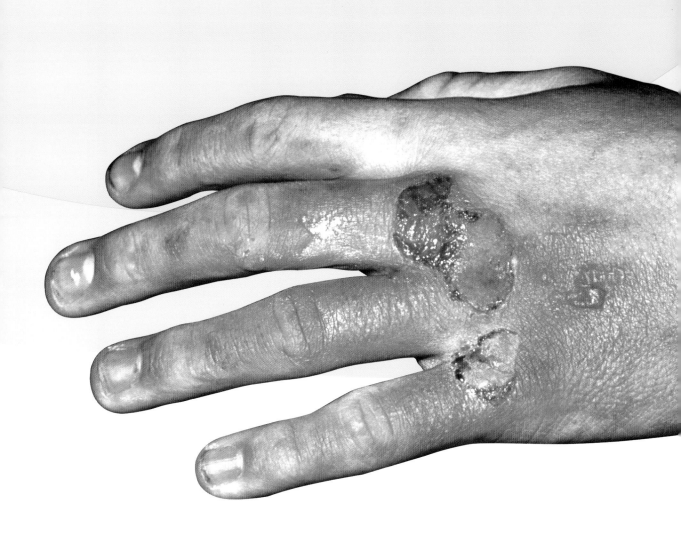

The size of the burn is important too. Large burns are more serious than small burns. Very serious burns can kill people.

Treating mild burns

If your skin touches something hot, the best thing to do is to cool it quickly. Hold it under cold running water for several minutes until it stops hurting.

If you **burn** your mouth or tongue, drink
some cold water to cool your mouth down.
Do not cover a mild burn with cream or with
a **dressing**.

Treating sunburn

If your skin is red and sore, you can rub in **after-sun cream**. This cream will soothe the soreness and help to stop your skin from becoming too dry.

22

When you have been **sunburnt**, you should cover your skin and keep out of the sunshine. Stay in a shady place until the **burn** has **healed**.

preventing sunburn

It is easy to prevent your skin becoming **sunburnt**. Rub **sun protection cream** into your skin before you go out. Make sure you include your face, ears, hands and feet.

Cover your head with a sunhat and wear a
T-shirt. Rub in more sun protection cream
every few hours. Remember, swimming
washes off suncream.

Treating serious burns

If you suffer a serious **burn**, you should go to a hospital or see a doctor. Serious burns are dangerous. They allow **germs** to get through your skin.

Serious burns can also lead to your body
drying out. A doctor will put a special
dressing on the burn. The dressing will help
the burn to **heal**.

Avoiding accidents and blisters

Stay away from hot things such as irons, cookers and barbecues. Remember that **electrical appliances** stay hot for a while after they have been turned off.

Avoid getting **blisters** on your feet by wearing thick socks with heavy shoes. Let your feet get used to new shoes before you wear them for a long walk.

Glossary

accident   something that happens by mistake

after-sun cream   cream that helps to soothe the skin and prevent it from drying out, when someone has been in the sun for too long

blister   bubble of liquid that forms at the surface of your skin when it has been burned

burn   what happens to your skin when it is damaged by something very hot

dressing   clean pad of cloth that is used to cover wounds

electrical appliances   machines that use electricity to work. An iron is an electrical appliance.

germs   tiny living things, such as bacteria, that can cause disease if they get inside your body

heal   when a damaged part of your body repairs itself

heel   back of the ankle joint

prick   make a small hole with a pin or other sharp object

scald   burn with steam. Steam can be hotter than boiling water.

steam   very hot droplets of water that float in the air

sun protection cream   cream that stops the sun burning your skin for a length of time

sunburn   red, itchy, sore skin that has been burned by the heat of the sun

More books to read

Body Matters: Why Do I Get Sunburn? And other Questions about Skin, Angela Royston, (Heinemann Library, 2002)

Look After Yourself: Healthy Skin, Angela Royston, (Heinemann Library, 2003)

Safe and Sound: Safety First, Angela Royston, (Heinemann Library, 2000)

Index

Titles in the *It's Not Catching* series include:

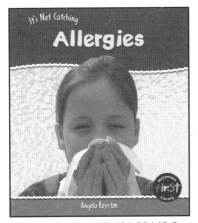

Hardback   0 431 02143 0

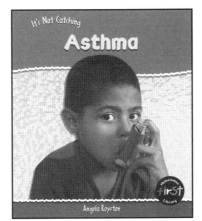

Hardback   0 431 02142 2

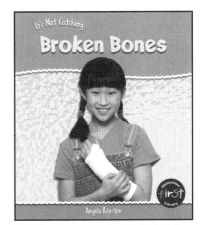

Hardback   0 431 02145 7

Hardback   0 431 02149 X

Hardback   0 431 02148 1

Hardback   0 431 02144 9

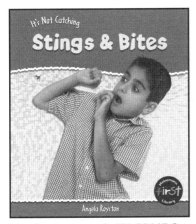

Hardback   0 431 02147 3

Hardback   0 431 02146 5

Find out about the other titles in this series on our website www.heinemann.co.uk/library